# solving conflict nonviolently

*This book is dedicated to you young people who have been bullied and have felt trapped between your desire for revenge and your desire to work things out peacefully. This book is also dedicated to you parents, teachers and counselors who want to help young people understand their violent feelings and cope with them in healthy, humane ways.*

## To the Reader:

I've written *Facing the Double-Edged Sword* to explore ideas, feelings, and aspects of training which are common to *all* Martial Atrs styles. My background is mainly in Japanese Karate, and I have used certain Japanese worlds such as *kiai, hara, hakama,* and *gi*—certainly not out of disrespect for other styles, but simply because they are the terms I am used to. You will see that this book has universal significance and is meaningful to all Martial Artists, whatever their style.

# FACING THE DOUBLE-EDGED SWORD

## *The Art of Karate for Young People*

by Dr. Terrence Webster-Doyle

Weatherhill
New York & Tokyo

A Martial Arts for Peace Book
published by Weatherhill, Inc.
of New York and Tokyo
in cooperation with the
Atrium Society
Middlebury, Vermont

First edition, 1988
First Weatherhill edition, 1998

Illustrations: Rod Cameron
Cover Design: Robert Howard
Design and Production: John Shoolery
Project Director: Game Plan, Inc.
Creative Consultant: Jean Webster-Doyle

Special thanks to Taki Name Do instructors:
Jeff Greene, Steve Snedden, Stan James, and
Jean Webster-Doyle

Library of Congress Cataloging-in-Publication Data

Webster-Doyle, Terrence, 1940–
Facing the double-edged sword: the art of karate for young people /
by Terrence Webster-Doyle [illustrations, Rod Cameron]
p. cm. – (Martial arts for peace series)
SUMMARY: An introduction to karate and other martial arts, with an emphasis on peaceful ways to deal with conflict. Audience: For grades 4–9.
ISBN: 0-8348-0465-4 (paperback)
1. Karate — Juvenile literature. 2. Martial arts — Juvenile literature
I. Cameron, Rod. II. Title. III. Series
GV1114.3    796.8153    QB191-147

Printed in Hong Kong

# Table of Contents

# There's a Fight Going On

You are out on the playground after school when you hear some kids yelling. As you run over to see what is happening, Robbie, one of your classmates, and a good friend, runs past you looking scared. You reach a group of kids standing at the far edge of the school playground, out of sight of any teacher's view. Someone is crying.

You move to the front of the group. You see Tom, your best friend, on the ground. There is blood on his face. His glasses lay broken beside him. Vinnie, the school bully, is on top of Tom holding him down. Martha, Tom's sister, is standing near them crying.

You remember at lunch earlier that day Vinnie pushed ahead of you and Tom in the food line. Tom asked him politely not to do that. Vinnie then pushed Tom and said that he would get him for "mouthing off."

You see your best friend lying there hurt and you wish you could do something to stop the fight. You feel helpless. As you start to move forward to do something, you suddenly feel a pain in your side. Eddie, Vinnie's best buddy, has just elbowed you and is now giving you a challenging glare.

You see that Vinnie is about to hit Tom again. Your stomach starts to hurt as you feel the pain Tom is experiencing. Your side aches also from where Eddie hit you. What can you do? You can run away like Robbie. You also feel like crying, but you fight to hold back the tears of hurt, anger and frustration. If you try to stop the fight Eddie will probably beat you up. He has threatened to do so in the past and is now waiting for the chance. You feel that your choices are not so great.

Have you ever felt like this?  Have you ever been picked on by a bully and felt angry and helpless?  Have you ever had to run away from a bully and felt ashamed?  This happens every day at most schools and in the community.  It also happens at home between brothers and sisters.  Most of you don't have many choices in coping with conflict.  Most young people can only run away or stand and fight, which usually means that the person getting picked on by the bully gets beaten up.  This means that you can get hurt physically if you try to fight against a bully or you can feel hurt emotionally if you run away.  Either way you lose.

The title of this book, <u>Facing the Double-Edged Sword</u>, was chosen because a double-edged sword has two sharp sides and can cut or hurt someone either way it is used.  This idea of the double-edged sword is like what can happen to you if you are picked on by a bully — you can either fight or run away.  These two choices are not helpful in solving the problem.  In "Facing the Double-Edged Sword" you will need to make more intelligent choices in dealing with conflict.  This is what this book is all about — how you can learn to successfully handle conflict in nonhurtful, nonviolent ways.

# INTRODUCTION

Hello. I am Chief Instructor Sensei (sen-say) Webster-Doyle. Sensei means teacher. I teach a certain kind of Karate called Take Nami Do (tah-kay na-me doe). I want to show you how you can handle a situation like the one you just read about in more creative ways than running away or getting beat up by someone like Vinnie. I have taught Karate for almost thirty years and have never forgotten what it was like when I was a kid growing up. I used to get beaten up a lot then. I was always so scared. There was one bully who used to pick on me a lot, and I teach Karate to kids now because I don't want you to be hurt like I was.

My style of Karate, Take Nami Do, is similar to most other Japanese styles in lessons about self-defense. What is different about what I do is that I teach you about yourself, and teach you how to stop a fight before it happens. I want to also teach you about violence — what it is and where it comes from — so that when you grow up, you will be a more peaceful adult.

I have written this book to offer you a chance to understand that there is more to a Martial Art like Karate than the physical self-defense skills you have seen on television, in the movies, or perhaps in your own Karate class. Studying self-defense skills can certainly help you feel confident if someone ever wants to fight with you. But Karate is much more than this. Karate has psychological skills. Psychology means understanding the "why" and "how" of a person. So, with regard to Karate, it means understanding why you want to take Karate and how Karate will help you feel happier about your life. I'll bet there are times in your life when you've wished you could be happier

about a lot of things. Well, I think that learning how to use your mind (psychology) to get out of a fight before it happens can make you happier in your life. In this book I talk about the many ways you can do this.

I am interested in helping young people stop conflict without hurting themselves or other people. I think it is important to help you understand your mind, so that you can see how it works, how sometimes people's minds make them feel unhappy, and even violent. The truth is that the mind is far more powerful than the fist or the foot.

This book will not teach you the self-defense skills of blocking, punching, kicking, and striking. These should be learned at a proper Karate school with a qualified teacher. We feel it is dangerous to show you how to fight just from a book. What we do want to show you is just as important and also lots of fun. Learning how to defend yourself is only a small part of Karate.

Most important, Karate teaches you how *not* to get into a fight. It teaches you how to be gentle. I have students just like you who really don't like to fight but who have felt that fighting was their only choice. Maybe you wear glasses and a bully calls you "four eyes." Maybe your build is small, and other kids pick on you. Maybe you're not that great at sports, and you're looking for something you can feel good at. Maybe you're a girl and you have been told that you're not as strong as a boy. Maybe you're just plain tired of being scared of somebody, and you're looking for something that will give you confidence. You've come to the right place.

I have written this book to help you understand yourself, which is the most important thing Karate can do for you.

# Chapter 1

# HOW KARATE BEGAN

*One day as Bofu, the well-known Japanese Karate teacher, was sitting carving a long stick, he was approached by Matsu, a famous Samurai (a Japanese warrior). Matsu exclaimed excitedly that he had finally understood the real meaning of true Karate (Kara...empty). He was finally empty, he said. He was free from his mind; he had attained real peace and nonviolence.*

*Expressionless, Bofu listened quietly for a few minutes as Matsu went on. Bofu suddenly whacked Matsu sharply on the head with his stick.*

*Enraged, the Samurai leaped to his feet and shouted, "You stupid old fool! That hurt! I could kill you for that!"*

*"My, my," said Bofu calmly. "This emptiness is certainly quick to show anger, isn't it?"*

*After a few moments, Matsu smiled sheepishly and crept away.*

— an Old Story

## "Empty Hands"

Karate, as it is generally known, means "empty hands."

Kara = empty    Te = hands

Can you guess why?  Over many centuries, Karate has developed into a system of self-defense without the use of weapons.  But Karate is more than this.  It is also a healthy physical fitness program — a means of exercise to keep your body in good shape. And even more, Karate is a means to understand and go beyond the violence and disorder we live with daily.

## Shaolin-szu or Kempo

The earliest record of the development of the Art of Karate began many hundreds of years ago when a famous Buddhist monk (one who follows the teaching of Buddha) named Daruma Taishi (Dar-u-ma Tie-she) traveled from India to China. When he was in China he stayed at a monastery (a religious dwelling) called Shaolin. Here he taught the monks (a group of religious people) about Buddhism. He also taught them a system of physical and mental self-defense techniques so they could keep themselves physically fit and at the same time defend themselves against bandits that attacked the monastery. This system became known as Shaolin-szu or Kempo, "fist way."

## Kung Fu

Kung Fu is another Chinese style of Karate. Its fighting techniques were taken from movements of such animals as the tiger, the crane, the monkey, the leopard, the snake and even the mythical dragon. Like any particular system of Karate, Kung Fu had its own unique set of techniques. It was practiced by only a few specially chosen students and was done in secret in order to protect it from falling into the hands of the wrong people.

"My, my," said Bofu calmly. "This emptiness is certainly quick to show anger, isn't it?"

# Karate

After almost a thousand years in China, Kempo and Kung Fu spread to other parts of the Far East — like Korea and Okinawa. In Okinawa, an island off the coast of China, Kempo and Kung Fu (Chinese Karate) were called "Karate" which meant "Chinese hands." It is fascinating how it developed. At the time it was a crime for common people to have any weapons, which were outlawed and allowed only to the military ruling class. The people began to develop parts of their bodies like weapons in order to protect themselves. The side of the hand (the Karate "chop") was used like a sword. The tips of the fingers were made hard and strong like a spear (spearhand). The bottom of a clenched fist was a hammer (hammer hand) or mace.

In Okinawa, in the late 1800's, there lived a man named Gichin Funakoshi. He was an elementary school teacher in his early life but gave up teaching to study Karate full time under two Masters of that period. He was already familiar with Karate and had been studying it since he was 11 years old. Funakoshi traveled to Japan in the early 1900's and introduced Karate to the Japanese. It quickly caught on and was sponsored by the Japanese Ministry of Education.

Funakoshi started the Japanese Karate Association and Shotokan (show-toe-kon), his own style of Karate, around 1948. In 1957 Funakoshi, now considered the father of modern Karate, died at the age of 88. He had spent 77 years studying and teaching this art form!

Currently Karate is enjoyed throughout the world. Wherever you may travel, Karate is known and appreciated. Although there are numerous fighting styles that have their roots in many countries, the best known come from China, Korea, and Japan.

## Empty Hands to Empty Self

In Japan, the meaning of Karate, "Chinese hands" evolved into "empty hands." This came about due to the philosophical aspect of Karate. Philosophy is the study and love of truth in daily living and, combined with the physical exercise of the body, makes for a *whole* being. The philosophical side of Karate comes from a religion known as Zen, which has its origins in Buddhism.

Zen says that life each moment is an ever-changing wonder, that every day is a miracle, because living is always new and fresh. Young children seem to see and live more simply than adults. Zen says that people lose the ability to be like a child as they grow up. Adults become too serious, afraid, worried. Their minds become overloaded with troubled thoughts. They become so worried that their minds fill up, like a cup of tea filled to the brim, so nothing else can get in. Adults are so concerned with feeling bad about the past and are afraid of the future that they cannot live in the moment — in the here and now. As a result, they cannot fully enjoy the natural world, the wonderful smell of the trees and flowers. They cannot listen to the rain falling on the roof, see the glory of birds in flight, experience the greatness of the ocean on a bright sunny, summer day — all the things children seem to naturally love and appreciate.

"Emptying" one's mind of "unnecessary" thoughts is at the root of Zen and modern day Karate. By "unnecessary," I mean those thoughts that frighten you or make you worry too much,

as if they were real.  Through Zen there are methods of "empty-ing" the mind of all unnecessary thoughts so that we are free to act more clearly and intelligently.

## Zazen

One method of emptying the mind is what is called Zazen, or "sitting meditation."  In Zazen a person just sits and watches his or her breathing.  It is very simple and also very hard.  It is simple because it is natural to just be quiet and let the mind rest and be still.  It is hard because your thoughts sometimes run wild, and cause temporary confusion and anxiety.  As you concentrate on your breathing, something which is constant and always there — your mind begins to quiet, and your unnec-essary thoughts slow down and eventually disappear.  When people discovered this about Zazen, they found it to be a won-derful thing.  In learning this form of relaxation and the ability to focus totally and completely on something so here-and-now as their  breathing, it changed the way they lived for the better.  They learned relaxation and focus.

In Karate, Zen plays two very important parts.  Karate, as you probably already know, consists of different kinds of move-ments — for example, the basics, which are blocking, punching, striking, and kicking — and Katas, which are dance-like art forms made up of a combination of self-defense techniques.  By concentrating not only on one's breathing during periods of Zazen meditation, but also on the Karate basics and Katas, a person can slow down and even stop unnecessary thinking.  This is especially important to do if one needs to be aware of an opponent.  Unnecessary thinking wastes time and energy and prevents a person from responding instantly to an attack.

On another and much deeper level, Karate helps a person "empty" himself of anger, hurt, and confusion — the kind of thinking that clouds the mind and causes it pain. Karate as "empty self" is meant to bring about a peaceful, clear, and sensitive outlook to one who practices it. It is therefore much more than a self-defense or a method of "empty hand" fighting. Karate is an art that helps develop a confident, gentle, yet powerful person — one who can live more joyfully in the world and, as a result, bring more happiness and well-being to others.

The following quote by Gichin Funakoshi clearly defines empty self:

"As a mirror's polished surface reflects whatever stands before it, and a quiet valley carries even small sounds, so must the student of Karate empty one's mind of selfishness in order to respond appropriately to anything one might encounter. This is the meaning of Kara, or 'empty' in Karate."

Chapter 2

# A GREAT MASTER OF KARATE

*He opened his umbrella quickly and held it over the back of his head as a defense from any blows that might come from behind.*

The following short story really happened in Gichin Funakoshi's life when he was a young man. Explained in his own book, <u>Karate-Do, My Way of Life</u>, it is retold here to make one very important point: that Karate is not a way to defeat an opponent but a way to overcome the enemy *without* fighting. This may surprise you, for on the surface it looks like Karate is a violent practice. The real Karate student or teacher knows that Karate is actually a way to gentleness and nonviolence. The following story of Funakoshi, a great teacher, who truly lived the Art of Karate, illustrates this point.

## The Danger of Pride

Funakoshi was just 13 years old when he walked down a long and lonely road on his way to a neighboring town. On his journey he came upon a group of young people on a grassy hillside who were in the midst of an exciting and challenging game of hand wrestling.

Since Funakoshi was quite fond of this sport, and felt confident in it, he stopped and watched for a time. Suddenly one of the young boys called to Funakoshi, "Hey, you! Come on and try

to beat us! But maybe you're afraid to take one of us on?" Another of the youths called to him and challenged him again.

Since Funakoshi didn't want to cause trouble he said, "Thank you, no; excuse me, but I have to go." He started down the path.

"Hey, you can't go!" A few of the boys ran up to the young Funakoshi.

"Scared? Running away?" jeered one of the group.

"Come on, kid, that's not polite to leave," said another.

Two of the boys grabbed Funakoshi's shirt and dragged him back to where the remaining boys were waiting. Funakoshi realized that, after having studied Karate for the last two years, he could have used his skills and made a fast escape, but instead he decided to try his hand at the contest. His first bout, with the weakest and youngest of the group, he won easily. His second opponent he also defeated with ease. He went on to win the next three challenges. Now there were only two left, and they both looked strong.

"All right," said one of the strong, large boys, "it's my turn now. You won't get away so easily. Are you ready to take me on?"

Funakoshi looked at these last two large boys. "I'm afraid I'm not; I've had enough, and I'm sure I can't beat you anyway." He excused himself. But the young boys blocked his way. One of the two boys grabbed his hand so Funakoshi had to take him on. Funakoshi won again. "Now I really must leave," he said. "Thank you." And he excused himself again.

This time they let him go, but as he began walking down the road away from the group he heard sounds behind him. That morning when Funakoshi had left home he had taken his umbrella with him as it had been raining. Now that the rain had stopped he was using the umbrella as a walking stick. He opened it quickly and held it over the back of his head as a defense from any blows that might come from behind.

As he reached his destination, Funakoshi was filled with regret and sorrow. He was ashamed that he had let himself enter that hand-wrestling competition. He wondered why he had done so. "Was it mere curiosity?" he asked himself. But the true answer came to him: It was his over-confidence in his strength, in his ability to defeat those other boys at a game he felt good at. It was, in other words, his pride. He felt he had let his Karate teachers down and violated the spirit of the Art of Karate.

As he told this story almost 75 years later, he still felt deeply ashamed, because the great teacher truly believed:

*"To subdue the enemy without fighting is the highest skill."*

# Chapter 3

# TAKE NAMI DO AND MUKUSO

*"Can you bend like the bamboo in the wind? Can you not hurt back even when you have been hurt?"*

## Take = Bamboo

In Japanese, "Take Nami Do" means Bamboo-Wave-Way. Can you imagine what this means? In the practice of self-defense, TAKE means to block — to stop an attack. Because bamboo is a strong, resilient plant, when the wind blows, bamboo bends. It yields to the strength of the wind and "goes with the flow." It bends, but it does not break. When the wind stops, the bamboo comes back to its original form unharmed.

When you have been hurt, there have probably been times when you wished you could be like the bamboo. What have you wished you could do? Duck or dodge? Get out of the way? Hit someone back? Because it didn't feel good when someone made fun of you, or hurt you in some way, your immediate instinct was probably to hurt that person back. And if you did strike back, chances are you still didn't feel good.

There is something else you can do! You can be like the bamboo. You can bend in the force of the wind — in other words, you can listen to the hurtful words, or avoid the punch instead of hurting back. You are probably saying to yourself, why would I want to do that? Why wouldn't I want to hurt that person back?

Try this with a friend, just for the fun of it. Ask your friend to make fun of you, and see what happens inside. How do you feel? What thoughts go through your head? What do you want to say to that person? Do you want to call him or her names? What do you want to do to that person? Do you want to hit him? Slap her? Ah, but here is the trick: To *not* do any of those things. The trick is to simply WATCH all of this as if it were a movie. The trick is to LISTEN to all your feelings but not act on them. Can you do this? This is how you do it. You and your friend can take turns.

1. Ask your friend to make fun of you.
2. Listen to the hurtful words.
3. Watch the hurtful feelings.
4. Let the hurt come up so that you can feel it.
5. Let the hurt go away.

This acting like the bamboo is a very important part of Karate and of life. People get into a lot of trouble when they feel hurt and try to hurt back. Can you see the importance of not hurting back? What do you think it is? Talk this over with your friends, your teacher, your parents.

## Nami = Wave

In Japanese, NAMI means Wave. In self defense, wave means the strong force of a punch, kick, or strike. Sometimes a person has to be strong. But being strong does not mean being a bully and hurting people. Being strong means not fighting back; it means finding some other less violent way to deal with conflict. NAMI also refers to the strong feelings and thoughts we have that sometimes surface when we feel hurt, sad, angry, or frustrated. It is often important to share these strong feelings and thoughts with the person who said or did something that caused those feelings inside us.

Of course there are times when we cannot, or do not want to, share these thoughts and feelings. This can be very frustrating. What can we do instead?

## Mukuso

As part of the Art of Karate, the Japanese teach Mukuso (Mock-so). Mukuso means to meditate — to watch your thoughts and feelings without doing anything about them — like being the bamboo. Sometimes with the eyes closed, sometimes with eyes open, you watch your feelings and thoughts come up, like bubbles in a glass of soda. One by one, your hurt feelings rise to the surface and disappear.

When you practice Take Nami Do and Mukuso and watch your thoughts and feelings float like clouds across the sky, you learn to discover where your hurt comes from. And if you discover where your hurt comes from, you are on the path to the greatest exploration of all in the Art of Karate: the discovery of the "Empty Self."

Here is a story that will show you what we mean. It's about Luke, who dealt with a bully and found his Empty Self.

"Hey, you! Punk! You with the four eyes. You look stupid," yelled Brian, a tall, rough-looking, red-haired kid.

He was yelling at Luke in the playground. The playground supervisor was on the other side of the yard and couldn't hear what Brian was yelling.   Luke got a queasy feeling in his stomach, a feeling he was used to but was not worried about any longer since he was taking Karate.   He remembered his Karate teacher saying, "Look, Luke, fear is a natural feeling.   Sometimes it helps you get out of trouble, like when you realize you've run out into the street without looking.   It helps you act quickly so you can prevent yourself from being harmed.   But fear can cause problems, like when it makes you act at a time you know you shouldn't."

"You heard me, jerk!"   Brian was coming across the yard towards Luke.

Luke felt the fear rise up inside him.   But this time, instead of running away from Brian, as he usually did, he stopped and looked at the fear.   He let the feeling come up but didn't act on it.   Luke turned in Brian's direction and stood very still, watching and waiting.

"So, you wanna fight me, shorty?   Is that it?" Brian continued to push.

Luke felt a sudden flare of anger rise up in himself but instead of acting out his anger, he just watched it.   He heard his teacher's words, "Be like bamboo, Luke.   Let the wave come up and crash on you.   Just bend with it, don't resist."

Suddenly Brian stepped forward.   Luke, looking up at the larger boy, stood his ground.   Although he noticed a slight weakness in his knees, he didn't let it bother him.   He felt fear, but, again, he just watched it come up like a wave, and then go. Luke noticed that Brian was unsure of himself now that Luke was taking a stand.

"Aw, you ain't worth it anyhow," Brian blurted out in disgust.   "You're a coward! You know I could beat you if I wanted."

"You may be right, " Luke replied calmly. "So why fight?"

At this, Brian turned away and went back across the schoolyard looking for someone else to pick on.

"Good for you, Luke," his teacher said when Luke told him what had happened that day. "You have learned the lesson well of the bamboo and the wave."

Luke's teacher rang the bell at the beginning of class and all the students sat down quietly in Mukuso. As they sat they just watched what was going on — inside and out. Luke saw that his mind was going over what had occurred with Brian. Little by little the thoughts faded as he sat.

When the bell rang again and it was time for practice, Luke got up quickly, his mind now ready and alert in the moment for whatever should happen.

## Practicing Mukuso

Find a comfortable place to sit, where you can totally relax for a few minutes. Then do the following:

1. Think of someone who or something that has been on your mind lately — your father, your mother, your teacher, your close friend, the kids at school, your homework. Pick just one thought.

2. Perhaps you might want to think about someone or something you feel angry or hurt about.

3. As you are sitting comfortably, close your eyes and look inside at your hurt or angry feelings. Don't do anything — just *watch*. Be like the bamboo.

28

4. Let those feelings come up like bubbles in a glass of soda. Watch how they disappear, without any effort! You don't have to do anything. What is important is to just watch. Try not to judge what you see. If you do, just watch that. The point is to let the thoughts come and go without ever acting on the fearful or hurtful thoughts.

5. Think about where that hurt or angry feeling came from, and think about how good it feels to have it go away.

Can you bend like the bamboo in the wind? Can you not hurt back even when you have been hurt?

## Chapter 4

# MIND LIKE MOON — MIND LIKE WATER

*"The mind is like a mirror. It grasps nothing, it expects nothing. It reflects but does not hold. Therefore, one can act without fear."*

Another important principle of the Art of Karate is called Mind Like Moon — Mind Like Water. It is a basic principle of all forms and styles of the Martial Arts and has more than one meaning.

## Mind Like Moon

Perhaps you are trying to figure out what it's like to have a mind like the moon. If you picture a full moon on a dark night, you know that moonlight shines equally on everything within its range. If your mind shines equally on everything within its range, it will be open and aware of all things. In the art of self-defense, it is important that you are constantly aware of all your opponent's movements. With an open mind you can be immediately aware of an attack and you can react without thinking to get out of the way of someone who is trying to harm you. Clouds blocking the light of the moon are like distractions which interfere with the correct and accurate response needed to defend oneself. Do you understand now?

But "mind like moon" is much more than a way to avoid an opponent's attack. It means that you must see and understand violence — you must have an open mind to why one would want to do you harm, and you must look at what causes the violence.

You would have to think about the hurt, fear, and anger that you feel when you are attacked. You would need to see the reasons why you yourself would want to hurt someone, and you must attempt to understand why you feel hurt. Once you begin to see why you feel hurt, you will begin to understand why someone else gets hurt and why that person might want to hurt back. Then you begin to see what hurt is and how it causes violence. By seeing the problem, you can respond with true understanding, so that you are not merely defending yourself against being attacked physically. Understanding all of this, you can respond with intelligence and choose a more nonviolent, creative way to handle your problem.

## Mind Like Water

Now that you have an idea of what it means to have a mind like the moon, perhaps you can guess what it means to have a mind like water. In the self-defense aspect of Karate, "mind like water" is a calm mind like the surface of undisturbed water. Still water, like a mirror, reflects exactly what is there, without any distortion. This state of mind allows you to see an attack and, at the same time, respond to it immediately and accurately. If any distracting thought is allowed to enter the mind, it will be like throwing a stone into the water. The opponent's movements will not be clear and therefore the response will not be quick enough. If the mind is filled with thoughts of attack and defense, it will not correctly understand what the opponent is trying to do. Such unnecessary thought could bring harm to both you and your opponent.

There is an even deeper meaning to "mind like water."

When the mind is like still water, or a mirror, it reflects what is there without judging it. If the mind is still, silent and deep, it sees exactly what is before it without thinking about what should or should not be, without being concerned whether something is right or wrong, or good or bad. Judging what you see is like stirring a stick in water — it only makes the water muddy. A mind that can understand and intelligently respond to the deeper causes of violence must be clear.

Once you achieve this clarity of a still mind, you are then capable of something very special called *insight*, which is the ability to see, understand and act immediately to handle a problem. In the physical aspect of Karate, this is the ability to act instantly to protect yourself when you are about to be physically attacked.

Here is a story about how Emily found her "mind like moon, mind like water."

Suddenly a fist struck Emily in the face and her eyes started to water. Her face stung with pain as the teacher stopped the match. It was a freestyle match in which fighting is controlled but real. Emily sat down wanting to cry but she fought back the tears.

"That must have hurt. I'm sorry," said John. The rest of the class at their Dojo (Karate school) was busy practicing Kata (the Karate forms) when the accident happened. Their teacher sat down next to Emily.

"Emily," her teacher asked, "what were you thinking of when you got hit?" Her teacher looked at her face and saw that there was no injury.

"How did you know that I was thinking about how good

John was at freestyling?" Emily responded in surprise.

"I didn't know what you were thinking. But I could see that you were distracted. You didn't block that punch. John didn't control his punch, either. Both of you seemed preoccupied with something other than what you were doing. Can you see what happens when you are not giving your attention to what is happening in the moment?"

John came over and sat down next to Emily and his teacher. "Sorry, Emily. I just lost it. I was trying too hard. I thought I wanted to really show how good I was and I forgot that you were there."

"Do you both remember the talk I gave to the class last month on Mind Like Moon — Mind Like Water? Can you see now how this accident happened?"

Emily thought back to that talk and remembered her teacher telling them about it.

"Mind Like Moon is being aware of all things equally like the moon shining on everything. When your mind is like the moon you are immediately aware of an attack and you can therefore react spontaneously to get out of the way. Thoughts of winning or losing are like clouds blocking the light of the moon. They are distractions that interfere with the correct response to what is happening in the moment."

Emily also remembered how her teacher had talked about Mind Like Water, how water reflects exactly what is there and that the mind must be still, clear and calm like water and reflect without distortion. "Throwing a stone into clear water causes ripples. These ripples are like disturbing thoughts in the clear mind. You can be hurt if you let thoughts interfere with your action."

Emily remembered how her teacher also mentioned that there were deeper parts to Mind Like Moon and Mind Like Water than just getting out of the way of an attack.

"When the mind is still and unclouded it can see to the depths of yourself and another. It can see where the attack comes from, it can see the hurt and anger just below the surface. Watch carefully and you will see the root of violence within. Just watch and do not be distracted by the ripple and the storm clouds."

Emily thanked her teacher and got up.

"May we begin again, Sensei (teacher)?" asked Emily as she bowed.

"Remember, Emily, there is only One Encounter — One Chance! When you become inattentive you are in danger."

John bowed to Emily. They both took their fighting stances.

"Kiai!" (a yell used in Karate to give strength to the technique) shouted Emily as her kick shot out, stopping just short of her target.

"Kiai!" shouted John as he jumped forward with a controlled punch to Emily's chest.

"Kiai!" Emily swiftly blocked John's punch.

"Yami," called their teacher (which means "stop" in Japanese Karate).

"Good, you are now Mind Like Moon and Mind Like Water. You have faced and met the challenge of One Encounter — One Chance. Be alert — always!"

Here is a simple exercise you can do to help you understand Mind Like Moon — Mind Like Water. Find a quiet place, at home or in your Dojo. Sit on the floor or use a chair if sitting on the floor is not comfortable. Keep your back straight and your head up. Look down at the floor in front of you. Breathe naturally, counting each breath. One — inhale, Two — exhale, and so on. Later, as you practice, you can count one for the total inhale/exhale. Count to ten and then begin over again at one. If you find that you've gone beyond ten just notice it and start over at one. Just watch your thoughts and be aware, but not distracted by the noises or movements around you.

As you do this for awhile you can stop counting your breaths and just sit. The object of this exercise is to let your thoughts calm down so that you are not distracted by them. Sitting quietly observing your thoughts, you can learn a lot about them — where they come from and how they affect your life.

You can sit for as long as you like. Start with one minute and then work up to perhaps five minutes. See what happens when you sit like this. It might help you to keep a notebook to write down what you observe while sitting. It is best to do this right after you stop.

This is a very simple exercise but one that is very important for self-understanding. If your Karate class doesn't sit, ask your instructor if you can. Most Karate classes do sit at the beginning and end of class.

# Chapter 5

# FOCUS AND KIAI

*"This Ki, this energy, hit the youth like a bolt of lightening and snapped his head back. At that moment the young man saw his knife for the first time and saw what he was really about to do."*

Perhaps you have heard the phrase, "The shortest distance between two points is a straight line." If you think about this, you know that it's true. This principle came out of the study of physics, which is a science of how things work. Keeping this principle in mind, you can see how, in Karate, a punch, strike, or kick will have its most powerful effect if it is done in a straight line. Japanese Karate depends on this approach.

Another scientifically sound method of achieving great strength is focus. Focus is a process of developing a powerful defense or counter-attack by a series of movements done in a certain order.

For example, do you know how to do a reverse punch? The fist is thrust straight out from the body and, at the same time, the hips are twisted towards the target in order to use the strength of the hips and trunk of the body to give more power to the punching arm. The body is relaxed but in proper form. Being relaxed and in proper form, the punch has great speed. As the fist nears the target its speed is increased to its highest point and at the moment of contact the muscles tense, the breath is exhaled sharply (to bring the large and powerful stomach muscles into play) and all one's energy is concentrated for an instant at the fist.  Then the body instantly relaxes, the breath is inhaled and one is immediately ready for the next movement.

## Focus

Focus is the ability to concentrate all the body's energy, through the correct Karate form, on a certain target, for an instant.

It is essential, also, to have the correct attitude, the mental strength of confidence, without which Karate would not have its tremendous power.  Both physically and mentally, focus is one of the most important elements in the art of Karate.

## Kiai

Kiai (Key-ah) is another important principle in Karate and the fighting arts.

Ki = energy      Ai = union

Therefore, Kiai means a union, or coming together, of energy.  Isn't it a perfect word to describe that piercing yell that is heard when a Karate-ka (a Karate student) completes a movement? It is done by a sharp breathing out and tightening  of the abdomen muscles in the Hara (the lower stomach).  So, this shout also gives strength to the block or attack.

Kiai is also mental.  The following is a story told by Terry Dobson, a skilled teacher of Aikido, which is another form of the Japanese Martial Arts that uses evading, throwing, and holding down techniques to stop an opponent.  The story illustrates the effect that Kiai can have, even from a distance.

When he was in New York City a few years back, Dobson witnessed a strange and near-fatal scene. While walking down 14th Street on a late autumn afternoon, he noticed two teenagers run out of an appliance store and down the street. One of the boys had a large TV set in his arms; the other boy was trying to get it into a shopping bag as they ran together. The TV was much larger than the bag, so they were having some difficulty. Just then, the shopkeeper ran out after them in hot pursuit. The shopkeeper was well-dressed in expensive clothes and jewelry. From across the street Dobson watched this chase scene. Since the TV was too big for the boys to carry and still run fast enough to lose the shopkeeper, the boys sat it down on the sidewalk. One of the boys ran across the street leaving his companion. The shopkeeper caught up to where the lone boy was standing by the abandoned TV set. The shopkeeper, not paying attention to the youth, bent over to inspect his property. As he did, he turned his back on the boy.

From across the street Dobson saw something happen. A change took place on the boy's face, and a look of rage suddenly appeared. The boy reached into his pocket and pulled out a knife. The blade flashed in the sun as he raised it above the shopkeeper's back.

Dobson was stunned by the violence that was about to be committed. Physically there was nothing he could do; he was too far from them and there was no time. In a few seconds the shopkeeper could be mortally wounded. Suddenly from a deep place inside Dobson, a silent scream raced upward from his belly to his head. "NO!" he shouted! In a split second, a great impulse of energy streaked from Dobson to that boy. This ki, this shout, this energy, hit the youth like a bolt of lightning and snapped the boy's head back. At that moment the youth *saw* his knife for the first time and *saw* what he was really about to do. In that moment of realization, he turned around, closed his knife and quickly walked away. The shopkeeper had not seen any of this. He was busy inspecting his property. His life was almost taken but he would never know.

This ki (from Kiai), this union of energy, can be called upon in times of emergencies. It seems to be a natural part of us. Through the practice of Martial Arts you can more easily summon this great power at will. In addition to being a power or energy that can give great strength to the performance of Karate techniques, it also gives unusual power and intensity to tasks of everyday life. For example, in other sports, or in dangerous activities like rock climbing or rushing down the rapids of a river in a boat, Kiai can be helpful in summoning great strengths to meet the challenges. Kiai has been known to help people survive in many emergency situations. Kiai has been called the "life source" — the source of energy that is in all things and moves all things. It has been given many names but it is common to all people. It is the life blood of the Art of Karate.

# Chapter 6

# POWER

*The secret of getting power is really very simple...Practice your form.*


There is a formula in Karate.  It is:

Attitude + Form = Speed = Power!

Most people study Karate to gain power, but at first they do not understand how to get it.  Many try hard to be powerful but usually end up quitting Karate after a short while because they do not have the power they wanted.  Unfortunately, they never understand what real power is.

## Attitude

Your attitude is simply the way you think.  If your attitude is to get power right away, perhaps because you are scared of being beaten up, or you want to be able to bully others, you will not stay with Karate long, because it will not be meaningful to you.  The proper attitude consists of thinking thoughts that help you, "emptying" your mind of unnecessary thoughts that hurt you, and practicing proper form, slowly and carefully.  Patience is a definite requirement.

# Form

Your form means how you block, punch, kick, or strike. The quality of your form is determined by how well you do these self-defense techniques. **In the beginning you cannot present good form and be powerful at the same time.** Practice your form with care and attention, without trying to be powerful. Just focus your energy on doing *each* movement correctly. As you practice your form, you will get better and faster. Then you will become powerful — without trying.

If you maintain the proper attitude and practice correct form, you will see what real power is. You will also begin to understand what Karate is all about and you will not give it up in frustration.

# Self-Understanding

Power also comes from understanding yourself, not just from being physically strong. The questions to ask yourself are:

1. Why do I want to take Karate?
2. Do I really want to learn?
3. Am I afraid of making mistakes?
4. Am I afraid of defeat?

Those people who can be defeated are truly powerful people, for they are the ones who learn and grow from their defeat.

The following story is about a young man named Miguel, who learned the true meaning of power when he didn't have it.

Miguel finished his warmup, doing 50 situps and 50 push-ups. His body felt strong. He had been working out with weights and felt confident of his strength. He felt his muscles growing, but he also felt stiff and tired, as if he had been working out too hard.

Today, however, he was participating in his final round of freestyle competition. Miguel got excited when he thought about winning. He had won all his bouts against his fellow students so far. His father had always told him that winning was all that mattered. Since he and his father worked out together, and his father had been in the Marines and a college football star, Miguel very much wanted to please him and be like him.

Miguel, however, also liked to dance. He had joined a dance class at school and at first was embarrassed that the class consisted mainly of girls, but he wanted to try it out and stayed with the class. He was afraid to tell his father about his interest in dance. He had tried to play football but found that it was too violent a game for him. When he suffered an injury in the tryouts, he decided it wasn't for him.

Although his father was unhappy about Miguel's decision, he urged Miguel to practice Karate so he could "be a man." Although Miguel signed up for his father's sake, he found that he really liked Karate. It was taught by an older man who was gentle and understanding and who helped Miguel see that the art of Karate was like a dance — and that appealed to Miguel.

Today, during Miguel's final round, he was unusually excited because his father was there to see him compete. He noticed that his stomach started to hurt. He was very nervous and felt conflict within himself. On the one hand, he loved

Karate and respected his Karate teacher and his teachings.  On the other hand, he respected his father, but was afraid of him.  He wanted his father's approval but he couldn't find it in his heart to compete the way his father wanted him to.  Miguel had worked very hard for this day, and now that it was here, he felt this conflict inside him.  He watched the other bouts with a mixture of excitement and anxiety.  He knew that his father was watching him.  And he knew that his father would only accept him as a winner.

Suddenly it was Miguel's turn.  He jumped up and came forward to the freefighting area.  He was ready, but tense.  He wondered who he would fight.  He had seen all the other boys compete before him.  A person came up behind and passed him.

"There must be a mistake!" Miguel thought, almost out loud, as the person turned to face him.  There before him stood Suki, a girl!  She was 16, two years older than he, and a higher rank — a brown belt — while he was a green belt.  She practiced in the evening adult class so he had only seen her a few times.  He couldn't believe it!  Why her?  Why a girl?  He felt his face redden.  How could he fight her?  Although he had sparred with girls before, he had never done it seriously.

"Bow, please," he heard his teacher say.  While thinking, Miguel bowed to Suki, and then both of them bowed to their teacher.

"Ready," their teacher called.  Miguel's mind raced with confused thoughts.  What will Dad think of me fighting a girl?  Should I go all out?  But before he could resolve his questions his teacher shouted, "Begin!"

"Point!" called his teacher.  Suki had immediately moved in with a round house kick and caught Miguel wide open.  He

looked at his father and then back at Suki. "OK," he thought, "girl or no girl, I must fight!" With that he jumped forward with all his might and attacked.

"Point!" his teacher called again. Suki had easily and effortlessly blocked his attack and counter-attacked, scoring again.

Miguel was shocked! He started to get angry and more tense. He had trained for so long and felt so strong. How could this girl score twice on him? Again he attacked. With a flurry of techniques he charged his opponent and again she easily and gracefully moved out of his way, moving effortlessly and lightly as she dodged his attacks. She didn't look strong, but when she moved her techniques were very powerful. He, in contrast, looked powerful. He had developed a strong body weightlifting and could deliver a powerful punch or kick. And yet he couldn't score on her!

For the full two minutes of the bout Miguel went all out, giving his opponent the best he could, to no avail. He felt stiff and awkward pursuing her. She made him look like a muscle-bound ape, falling all over himself trying to capture a hummingbird. Just before the call to end the bout, Miguel felt his feet go out from under him as he tried one final and hopeless technique in an attempt to score. With all his might, with all the muscle and strength he could muster, he shot out a strong front thrust kick. It was like kicking the wind, and he fell forward in an off-balanced attempt.

Miguel got up, stunned but not hurt. Suki was standing in the ready position in front of him. She didn't even look tired, while he was sweating and out of breath!

She smiled at him, not a smile of victory, but one of

understanding. He knew he had been beaten, not by her as much as by himself. And she knew it, too, from her smile. He saw how his attitude had beaten him, how he thought that brute strength alone could win. He wanted to be powerful, to physically compete and dominate, and he learned that this idea of power wasn't useful in freestyle. That, in fact, it got in the way. Real power was agility, gracefulness and relaxation. Suki had wonderful technique. She didn't have weight training or muscular strength, but she had excellent form. Miguel's muscular power simply became useless with Suki.

Miguel looked at Suki and he, too, smiled. He realized the truth of her smile and understood one of the basic principles of the Art of Karate his teacher had talked about. "Real power not only comes from form, from being relaxed and gentle, but from understanding yourself, and knowing how to learn from defeat."

Miguel bowed deeply to his teacher and to Suki. He understood something important. The real lesson was in learning who he was. Realizing this, he knew he had "won" and would always be a "winner," even if he lost the bout. Now he could face his father as a "winner," knowing that the real victory was in learning what he had learned that day.

# Chapter 7

# SEN-NO-SEN: AWARENESS

*"What is important to learn in the Art of Karate is the Art of stopping conflict before it hurts you or another."*

Sen-No-Sen = Awareness of an attack before it happens.

You know how it takes time to learn a new sport or how to play a musical instrument. Achieving Sen-No-Sen takes practice too, in order to be good at it, but it takes no time at all to do if you are really aware.

## Listening to Feelings

Have you ever "felt" that something bad or dangerous was going to happen? Even though everything around you seemed calm? Sometimes, if we are really aware, we can sense when there is something wrong. Most of the time we don't listen to these "feelings" and just go on our way. But these feelings can be signals that something is not right.

There is nothing mysterious about having feelings that tell us that something isn't right. If you look closely at these feelings you will most likely see where they come from. What is probably happening is that you are sensing what is called "vibrations." These vibrations are disturbances in another person that haven't yet come out as physical action.

Here is an example that may have happened to you. You

are talking to someone and although you see that he or she is smiling, underneath the surface of the smile there is a feeling or vibration of anger, or hurt, or sadness. This is because the person is distracted — in two places at once. That person is talking to you, but is thinking of something else. That person's attention is divided between you and the troublesome thoughts he or she is experiencing.

Perhaps you have never thought about this before, but these troubled thoughts usually come from the past, from something else that happened to that person before — something that he or she did not fully understand. When we don't understand something that happens to us, we keep thinking about it — even though it happened in the past. When we do this we are in conflict. It hurts to be in conflict, because we want to be finished with what happened in the past and be able to be in the present.

## Watching Feelings

Sometimes our bodies show the conflict we are in. You may notice people wiggling their feet, rubbing their hands, tapping their fingers, squirming nervously in their chairs, or pacing. When you see this, you are aware of the other person's inner feelings, which are being expressed by body movement. This is called "body language." It is a language without words that tells you something about the person.

The kind of hidden conflict we have just mentioned will most likely not cause you any problems if you happen to see it in another person. But sometimes hidden conflict can affect you, even if you have nothing to do with it being there.

Sometimes you will sense that another person may feel hurt or angry and want to take it out on you. With Sen-No-Sen, you can stop this before it happens.

## Creating Distractions

There are several different ways to stop someone from wanting to attack you. Whether physically or verbally, the idea is to distract the person — to take his or her mind off what he or she is thinking. Can you think of ways to do this?

1. Change the subject of the conversation, if you feel whatever you are talking about is making the person angry.
2. Make a joke. Humor is a great way to distract a person. Make sure it is not an insulting joke. Laughter is very powerful. Sometimes it will cure the problem and sometimes not.
3. Get up and leave.
4. Try to be friends with the person and to help him or her find out why he or she is angry or hurt. This takes some practice. If you cannot come up with a good way to do this, you might want to ask an adult for help.

The important point here is that the Art of Karate is the art of stopping conflict before it hurts you or another. If you see conflict about to happen, just know that you can use your brain to stop it. Remember, the real test of a Martial Arts master is to end fighting before it starts.

# Fight, Flight or Freeze

Has anyone ever come up to you wanting to fight? What did you do? If it has never happened to you, what do you think you would do? Fight? Run away? Freeze?

Write down on a piece of paper what you did, or what you think you would do if this happened to you. If you fight, you go against the real test of a Martial Artist since you have not been able to end the fighting before it starts. If you run away, although you are happy to get away, you don't feel good about yourself for running. Furthermore, you haven't solved the problem. That person will probably confront you again. If you freeze, you are probably very afraid, which is natural, but freezing doesn't help your situation either.

Is there another way to deal with a person who wants to harm you? Write down, on your piece of paper, other ways you can think of to defend yourself.

We teach our students self-defense skills in Karate to help them feel confident in fighting. But we don't want them to fight! We teach them to fight so they have the confidence *not* to fight. Does this make sense? If not, talk it over with someone you trust, for it is an important point to learn.

When we teach you to defend yourself, we are actually teaching you how to *stop* a fight. The reason you become able to stop a fight without fighting is that you are not afraid — or, at least less afraid — of the other person. Can you see that if you have confidence because you know how to defend yourself, you don't have to fight? You don't have to prove anything to anyone, because you know you are strong.

53

Let's look more closely at the ways to stop a fight through nonviolent means. Remember that a true student of Karate is a gentle person — one who always *intends* to end a fight by nonviolent ways. This is the way to real power and real strength. If, however, you have no choice, and you must fight, hopefully you can do it in a way that is not harmful.

# Chapter 8

# WALKING AWAY WITH CONFIDENCE: POWERFUL WAYS TO AVOID CONFLICT

Here is a list of twelve ways you can solve conflict nonviolently. There are probably many more ways. Perhaps you, your friends, your family, or your teacher can think of others.

1) **Make Friends:** Treat the bully as a friend instead of an enemy. I don't know a bully who doesn't need admiration and respect.

2) **Use Humor:** You can turn a scary situation into a funny one. But be careful! Just don't make fun of the bully!

3) **Trickery:** Pretend you are sick. Pretend you have poison oak and that if you fight with the bully he will get what you have. Tell the bully someone is about to meet you. Pretend to faint.

4) **Walk Away:** Don't get into it. Just walk away. This is a simple and often overlooked way to end conflict before it begins.

5) **Agree:** If a bully insults you, agree with him. Even if you feel insulted, let your anger rise up and let it go. Just agree with the bully and see what happens.

6) **Refuse to fight:** This probably sounds contrary to what you have always been told, but one way to stop a conflict is to just not fight, no matter what happens.

7) **Stand Up to the Bully:** This can work, but it can also make the bully angrier. You must decide if you think this alternative will work.

8) **Scream/Yell:** A good shout or yell (Kiai) can shock the bully and distract him/her for a moment so you can get away.

9) **Ignore the Threats:** This is similar to simply walking away. You hear the threats and you turn and walk away from the bully, even though the bully is calling you a coward and trying to get you angry enough to react.

10) **Use Authority:** Call a teacher, a police officer, a parent, or someone you know who can help stop the bully from hurting you.

11) **Reason With the Bully:** If you are a good talker, perhaps you and the bully can talk it out. If you don't argue or get angry, if you act friendly, you might convince the bully not to hurt you.

12) **Take a Karate Stance:** As a last resort, you can take a strong Karate combat stance. This tells the bully that you are prepared to protect yourself if you are attacked. But hopefully, one or more of the other suggested ways to end the conflict will work.

When using one or more of these alternatives, it is important to remember:

1. Use an alternative and then move away from the bully as soon as possible.
2. Don't stand there and argue with a person who is threatening you.
3. Distract the person from wanting to hurt you and then get away.
4. Look for a nearby house to walk up to as if you lived there, or look for an adult to help you.

It is important to talk to your friends, family, and teachers about these alternatives and to practice with them. In the chapter that follows, we will talk about practicing these ways to end conflict so that you are more fully prepared in the event you are approached by someone that may want to do you harm.

# Chapter 9

# NONVIOLENT ALTERNATIVES

*"If in my younger days I had been in a fighting situation, I would have attacked first to take my opponent by surprise. Now I have learned, while remaining calm, to look for a solution that would leave everyone uninjured...yet I am still convinced that my power and skill are of such a level that I would not lose to any bully."*

— Shigero Egami
Chief Instructor, Shoto-Kan Karate
from <u>Heart of Karate-Do</u>

You know by now that the main purpose of learning Karate self-defense techniques is to give you confidence so that you know you could win a fight if you needed to. If you have this confidence, your mind is clear and free from fear. When your mind is clear and fearless, you are able to find creative, nonviolent ways to "win," which means never having to fight. This is called "winning by losing" or "win/win," because in this situation, everyone wins, nobody loses and, if you have to fight, nobody gets hurt.

## Roleplaying

Nonviolent alternatives are skills. They need to be practiced so you can become good at them. You might want to practice with a friend, one of you taking the part of the bully, and the other the part of the victim (the person being picked on). This is called roleplaying, because you are playing certain roles. It is important for you to have the chance to play both the bully and the victim. Can you guess why? Not only do you learn how to get out of a possibly harmful situation by nonviolent means, but you also get the chance to experience what it feels like to be a bully. Knowing what it feels like to be a bully can help you understand why a bully picks on people. This will help you in two ways:

1. You will know how to respond to the bully.
2. You will have compassion or sympathy for the bully and understand what he or she may be feeling inside.

Therefore, instead of reacting out of hurt, fear, or anger, you will act intelligently and creatively. Together with correct and strong Karate technique, you bring harmless, gentle skills to a potentially violent situation and are better equipped to produce a peaceful solution.

## Making Friends: A Roleplay Example

The following is a conversation between a bully and a victim. Find a friend to play one of the parts, while you play the other.

*Bully:*        *(Comes up to victim at school)*
"Hey, you! That's my seat. Move, dummy, or I'll pulverize you.

| Victim: | (Immediately thinks of Bully's name.) |
|---|---|

"Oh, hi!  Hey, I know you!  Aren't you George Klondike?"
*(The victim is trying to distract the bully and make
the bully forget his hostile intention)*

| Bully: | "Never mind who I am, shorty.  I heard you think you're hot stuff, a real champ." |
|---|---|
| Victim: | "I've always wanted to meet you George.  I think we have a lot in common.  I saw you riding a bike.  I really like bike riding." |
| Bully: | "Don't change the subject!" |
| Victim: | "Look, I really don't want to fight.  I'm not a fighter and I'm sure you can beat me.  You can have the seat.  I'd rather just be friends.  Why don't you come over and maybe we can ride together sometime." |

> *(Here the victim takes the energy out of the bully's
> hostility by admitting that he doesn't want to fight
> and would rather give up his seat.  The victim keeps a
> calm and friendly attitude in order to not make the
> bully angrier.  If the victim doesn't give the bully
> anything to react to, the bully probably has no reason
> to fight.  The victim stays "empty" of fear or anger and
> therefore does not react to the bully's threats.)*

How did it make you feel to play the bully?
How did it make you feel to be the victim?

You can talk about this with whomever you roleplayed with, and you can write your thoughts and feelings down on a piece of paper.

# Staying "Empty": A Roleplay Example

Here is another chance to roleplay a bully/victim situation. If you played the bully last time, switch parts, and this time play the victim.

*Bully:* "Hey, stupid punk, you're sitting in my seat!"

*Victim:* "I'm sorry. I guess I am. I won't do it again."

*Bully:* *(One type of threat.)*
"You do that again, and I'll punch you good."

*Victim:* *(Victim distracts bully by making friends.)*
"Listen, I'm new at this school, and I don't know my way around yet. Maybe you can help me."

*Bully:* *(Another type of threat.)*
"Oh yeah? Well maybe you can help *me*! Give me your money."

*Victim:* *(Victim uses trickery.)*
"Be careful! Don't touch me. I got poison oak this weekend. If you touch me, you could get it too!"

*Bully:* *(Another type of threat.)*
"You sound like a real brain, kid. Give me your homework!"

*Victim:* *(Another alternative.)*
"I'm sorry. I already turned it in. Besides, I can't do your homework for you, because that isn't honest. But maybe I can help you do yours. Let's meet in the library today and talk about it. Maybe we could help each other."
*(Victim uses reasoning or talking it out combined with trying to make friends.)*

*Bully:* *(Another threat)*
"Look, creep. I'm getting tired of your talking. Let's fight."

| | |
|---|---|
| *Victim:* | *(Another alternative — Victim stands up to the bully.)* |
| | "Okay, but I need to warm up first." |
| | *(The victim steps back and goes through a few warm-up self-defense techniques of Karate, snapping out some powerful punches and kicks.  Seeing this, the bully has second thoughts.)* |
| *Bully:* | "Aw, you're taking too long, punk.  I'm going!" |

Remember, this is only make-believe.  These stories are not real, but they could be and they could happen to you.  It would be good for you and your roleplaying partner to make up your own situations and responses to fit your own needs.  Do you think you can do that?  Practicing these responses over and over again, like practicing Karate self-defense techniques, will ensure that you are not caught by surprise.

Remember!  You do not have to act out of fear, because:

1. You *can* do something about being bullied.
2. You do *not* have to be a victim.
3. You do *not* have to fight.
4. You can use your *brain* instead of your *brawn*.
5. Your mind is a far greater weapon than your fist or foot.

But in order for all of this to work for you, you must constantly exercise this endless source of power called your mind.  If it's going to be ready to use when necessary, it has to be in good shape.

# Chapter 10

# KARATE MANNERS

*"Do for others as you would like them to do for you."*

I know that your family and your teachers have probably talked to you a great deal about the importance of good manners. You have perhaps come to believe that practicing good manners is something you *should* do. I would prefer that you think of them as something you *want* to do. After all, having good manners is being kind and caring for others, and we all want to be treated kindly and in a caring way.

In the Art of Karate, it is important to act as a "gentleman" or "gentlewoman." This means you learn how to act politely not only at home and at school, but also in the Dojo (the Karate school).

1. You learn how and when to bow.
2. You learn to address your Instructor as Sensei (sen-say) — the Japanese word for "teacher."
3. You learn to be polite to your fellow students.

These rules and others make for a good relationship between students and teachers, and students and students.

# Bad Manners

Some examples of bad manners are:
1. Rushing around and pushing or shoving to get in front of a line.
2. Interrupting someone while he or she is talking.
3. Dumping your shoes and clothes on the floor of the Dojo changing room.
4. Calling someone a name because he or she wears glasses or is tall, or short, or from a foreign country, or a different color.

Ask yourself how you feel when others are being bad mannered. How do you feel when you are using bad manners?

# Good Manners

1. Letting someone in line without pushing or shoving.
2. Greeting your teacher and fellow students with respect.
3. Holding a door open for someone.
4. Saying "thank you" when someone holds a door open for you.
5. Waiting until someone is finished talking before speaking.

Good manners are the foundation of the practice of the Art of Karate, just as a good foundation is essential for the building of a strong house. Manners make it possible for people to have intelligent and happy relationships. But, just like self-defense techniques and alternatives to fighting, manners must be practiced. As you practice them, ask yourself from time to time why they are important.  When you truly see the need for them, good manners will come naturally, from the heart.

In Take Nami Do Karate, we have a saying.  It goes like this:

"We ask our young students to put their shoes by the entrance of our place of practice. They line them up just so, taking care to observe the order in this simple gesture.  They think that Karate is punching and kicking.  We know that the Art of Karate is lining up their shoes — just so."

— Terrence Webster-Doyle
from  <u>Karate -The Art of Empty Self</u>

# Chapter 11

# HOW TO CHOOSE A KARATE SCHOOL

Karate is a way of life that teaches the importance of choosing carefully.  The selection of the right Karate school requires that you make a careful choice.  There are many different kinds of Karate schools, and you must sometimes visit more than one to find the right one for you.

I think that it is important to see how the instructor teaches so you can see what kind of person he or she is.  If the instructor is interested only in teaching self-defense, then you will only be taught how to fight.  If the instructor is interested in helping you understand yourself and interested in helping you end conflict by nonviolent means, then, in my view, he or she is teaching Karate in a helpful way — a way that will help create peaceful relationships between people.  My advice is to use the following checklist as you visit schools and observe classes:

1. Ask the students what they think of the classes.
2. Observe the classes for yourself.
3. Ask the teachers many questions and observe how they respond to your asking questions.
4. Ask if you can try a class or two.
5. Be aware of the "vibrations" you get from the instructors.  Are you afraid?  Do you feel you can trust them?  Listen to your feelings.
6. Ask how much lessons cost and what the payment

schedule is.

7. Look around at all the options. Don't feel pressured into taking lessons at one particular school.

Trust what you see and feel. If you take your time, you will find the right teacher and school. Choose with care.

# Chapter 12

# FIGHTING THE INVISIBLE ENEMY

*"To Subdue the Enemy Without Fighting is the Highest Skill"*
— Gichin Funakoshi

You have probably seen a lot of war and Martial Arts movies, either on television or at the theatre. Perhaps you have seen pictures of fighting in magazines as well. This is what I call "visual violence." Rather than real acts of violence, pictures or images of violence are presented to us in glamorous ways. The people who make these films and put out these magazines believe that showing you these images will not harm you. I do not agree. I believe that watching violence creates more violence. I think that those images of violence you see *do* harm you because they make you feel afraid — as if you were surrounded by enemies you must learn to fight.

Are these particular enemies real? Can they actually hurt you physically? Or are they simply "invisible" enemies — images you create in your mind? If you have ever awakened from a nightmare in which a "bad" guy or unknown enemy was after you, have you wondered where those images came from?

If you are a regular television watcher, by the age of 18, you will have sat in front of that set for over 15,000 hours! If you watch that much TV, did you know that you will have seen over 18,000 murders, not to mention all the beatings, muggings, and other forms of violence? Do you believe you can watch this much violence without being affected by it in some way?

73

The reason I am concerned about this is that I, too, grew up watching violence on television and in movie theatres, as well as reading it in magazines. I watched so many war movies that I dreamed of being old enough to be a soldier so that I could use guns and other weapons. I also used to play "cowboys and indians" with my friends. We played the game the way we saw it on television: the cowboys were always good and the indians were always bad. We cowboys pretended to kill the indians because they were the enemy. Television and movies taught us to believe this.

In addition, we had comic books that showed us super-heroes battling terrible enemies. We were excited by those battles and secretly wanted to be like those heroes, because television, movies and magazines made battles and violence look appealing. The truth is that such battles are anything *but* glamorous. People are hurt and killed.

This is why I am concerned about how the violence you see will affect you. The message I want you to get from this book is different from the one you get from those movies and TV programs. We cannot stop violence by showing violence that has been created to look good and right. The only way to end violence is to *not be* violent.

What can you do to not be afraid of those violent images? You can start by making yourself aware of how watching these violent pictures affects you. If you need assistance, please ask a trusted friend, parent, or teacher to help you do these simple activities. After watching a violent movie, reading a scary book, or awakening from a nightmare, if you find that you are frightened:

1. Sit in a quiet place in mukuso (see Chapter 4). Allow the images to come up in your mind. Don't do anything about them. Just *watch*. Let them come up and go. If you need to, count your breaths 1 to 10 and over again as you watch. This helps calm the mind.

2. As you begin to see these images, watch them as if your mind was a movie screen. Don't call them fearful or joyful or happy or sad. Try to look at them without any emotion. Realize that images are *only* moving pictures and that they are not going to hurt you.

3. If a particular image really bothers you, don't avoid it. Face it. If it is too scary, first look at another less scary image.

4. Realize that you have control over these images. Here's a fun thing you can do to make a really scary image, such as a bad guy, not scary.

    • Talk to the bad guy. Tell it that you are not afraid. Tell it a joke to make it laugh.
    • See if you can change the image in your head. If it is really big, make it small. If it has a scary look on its face, make it smile. Make it dance, or make it hug you.

You will be surprised to find out that you have control over these images; the more control you have, the less they will have over you.

Something else you can do is practice Karate with an understanding teacher who can help you develop the confidence not only to stop fights with real bullies without violence, but also help you make peace with any invisible enemy you have in your mind.

Studying the Art of Karate not only offers us the opportunity to learn a physical self-defense, which gives us confidence to end physical violence, but also provides us with an understanding of the psychological violence within us, so that we can talk about the violent images in our minds — what they are, how they got there, and what to do about them. This is the real challenge in Karate!

Chapter 13

# THE NEW WARRIOR
# MASTERING THE ART OF BUDO

Did you know that modern day Japanese Karate comes from the Art of Budo? Budo, or Bushido, was an ancient warrior's code, which meant "the way to stop the sword." In wartime, people had to protect themselves from being hurt by the sword, which was the weapon commonly used to kill people. Many people who practiced the Martial Arts were peaceful and did not want to hurt other people, so they practiced forms of weaponless combat in order to be able to defend themselves against attack. Like you and me, they also felt that defense was not enough; they wanted to find a way to end conflict so people would no longer get hurt. So they expanded the meaning of Budo to mean "to stop conflict." They were serious about ending all conflict in their lives and living without violence.

These early nonviolent Martial Artists understood that there were many forms of conflict and violence. They raised their children nonviolently by showing them what they felt was hurtful to other human beings, as well as to other living creatures. They felt a great love for nature and all living things, and felt that it was wrong to kill animals for food or sport. They became what we call today "vegetarians," people who don't kill or eat the flesh of animals. They ate natural foods such as grains, vegetables and fruits, and were very healthy.

These earlier nonviolent Martial Artists have helped

In bowing you forget yourself. Then you can greet one another because you are not the most important.

today's Martial Artists understand the real purpose of Budo — which is to stop conflict.  We live in a terribly violent world with constant wars.  Today we need a "new warrior," one dedicated to peace.  We must question why conflict and violence exist  and how to remove them from our lives.  We must ask ourselves, isn't it still important to not hurt animals for any reason, not to kill them for food or sport?  Isn't it important to live without weapons, even toy weapons?  Isn't it possible that playing with war toys when you are young can lead to a desire to use real guns in real wars when you become an adult?

What types of conflict are you aware of in your life or in the lives of people you know?

I have seen my Mother in conflict over_____.
I have seen my Father in conflict over _____.
My best friend has had a conflict with _____.
The most conflict I have in my life is _____.

Ask yourself what you think each of those people, including yourself, could do to become a peaceful warrior and bring peace to their life and to the lives of others.  What steps do you think could be taken in your home, at school, in your Dojo, and in the community to stop conflict?

By thinking through these questions and taking the time to come up with some answers, perhaps discussing them with friends and family, you are already in the process of becoming a more peaceful person.  Keep in mind that a real master of Karate not only masters the physical act of self-defense, but far more importantly, masters the art of living a healthy, happy, peaceful life, free from conflict.

# A SPECIAL NOTE TO THE YOUNG READER

Thank you for reading this book. I hope that you have enjoyed it and that it helps you learn more about yourself and what it means to "solve conflict nonviolently." I wish you well in your practice of the Art of Karate. If you don't practice Karate, I hope that this book will help you anyway.

If you would like to write me and share your stories about how Karate has helped you, especially how you got out of conflict through nonviolent ways, I would greatly appreciate it. This will help me write other books for young people. Maybe one of your real life stories could help someone else.

The last section of this book is written for adults so they too can understand the importance of solving conflict nonviolently through the Art of Karate. You can read their section if you want to. If you need the assistance of an adult to do so, be sure to ask. If you would rather stop here and think over what you have just read, that's okay too. Either way I thank you again for being such a good listener.

With affection and respect,

Terrence Webster-Doyle, Sensei

I leave you with this one last observation,
*"Drinking Green Tea*
*I stopped the war."*

— Paul Reps

Do you understand? Let's talk about it.

# A Message to Parents, Teachers and Counselors

This is an important message to anyone who works or lives with young people. The fundamental intention of this book is to teach young children how to cope with conflict in healthy, nonviolent ways.* This is not a book that teaches self-defense. It teaches young people to:

1.  Gain an understanding of the causes of violence
2.  Develop the skills to resolve conflict nonviolently
3.  Have the confidence *not* to fight

The idea of teaching conflict resolution skills to young people is vitally important. Yet it is almost totally overlooked. As a parent of five daughters, an educator/psychologist and someone who has worked in juvenile delinquency prevention, I am acutely aware of the violence our children are exposed to every day. I am also aware that there is little being done to help young people cope with the fight or flight situations they are confronted with at their schools and in their communities.

There is a tremendous amount of violence in our world, as anyone can see — on television, in films, newspapers and magazines — and it is all too often portrayed as an heroic cultural ideal, depicting fighting as the honorable solution to conflict. Violence is epidemic. It touches every life. The threat of nuclear war is a very real possibility. Our children live in a world of constant violence, perhaps the most violent time in the history of mankind. According to recent statistics, a violent crime occurs every 25 seconds. This is not a doomsday statement but a very real fact! In the glaring reality of global violence and in an age in which we have put a

---

*There are many more benefits in learning Karate. Coordination, strength, agility, timing, and flexibility are excellent physical fitness benefits not only for toning the body but, as research has shown, also helping the young person enhance intellectual, academic learning. Karate is also an exciting and challenging recreational sport, one that emphasizes individual accomplishment within a group context.

man on the moon, we still carry on as if there is nothing we can do.

It seems to me that what we need to do first is see that we parents, teachers and counselors *can* deal with the problem of violence especially when it comes to our children. The myth that only the authorities can deal with this issue is our biggest block to taking action ourselves. The second thing we need to do is teach ourselves and our young people the necessary skills to resolve conflict. In order to learn these, we need to understand what causes our conflicts and how we can fundamentally deal with them.

The title of this book, <u>Facing the Double-Edged Sword</u>, is a metaphor for the fight or flight survival mechanism in the deeper recesses of our brains. You may have experienced this fight or flight mechanism at one time or another in response to a threat to your survival. If you have a cat or dog, you have seen your pet react when confronted by a threat. The animal reacts according to this built in survival mechanism by either attacking (fight) or running (flight), depending on the specific conditions.

The human fight or flight mechanism reacts in the same mode as that of the animal in certain circumstances. When, for instance, a young person is confronted by a bully on the playground, the victim usually has only this flight or fight option available to him or her. The brain relies on this more primitive mode of dealing with hostile aggression because it hasn't been shown anything else. Adults generally only reinforce this method of dealing with conflict by telling the young person to either fight or "turn the other cheek."

If we are truly concerned about our childrens' welfare as they grow up we must take the issue of conflict resolution seriously and offer our children better options. If we want to bring about a safe and peaceful world we must help them develop alternative methods to our instinctual primitive reactions to threat. The terrible violence that is going on in the world today, the thousands of years of wars we've suffered, I believe, is stimulated at least in part by our primitive fight or flight animalistic behavior.

We must help young people understand and creatively, non-destructively deal with conflict. We educate young people in math, science, language, history, sports, and a multitude of other subjects. Why not conflict resolution?

A few concerned adults who have addressed this issue of teaching conflict resolution to young people have made good beginnings. Some have tried to show young people intellectually how to get out of conflict. For example, some teachers have demonstrated ways of talking one's way out. Others have taught children to defend themselves physically in the hopes that this would deter a bully's attempt to hurt them. What we rarely have done is to combine the two — the intellectual with the physical. Together, they provide a holistic approach to solving conflict.

Many people resist teaching young children to defend themselves since they think that violence only breeds violence. If self-defense is all that is taught then the outcome may well be only violence. But if the young person is also taught nonviolent alternatives to conflict (through role-playing) then the child is capable of coming up with more creative ways to deal with a potentially hostile situation.

This is how it works: The skills of physical self-defense give the young person confidence. This confidence assures him or her that he or she can handle a potentially violent situation. The acquisition of these skills circumvents the primitive fight or flight mechanism. If, in a potentially threatening situation, a child has been taught to defend him or herself, the message to the brain does not immediately stimulate an animalistic reaction. Instead of fighting or running away one can pause in readiness. In the "pause" there is a moment of calm, an abatement of the fear that stimulates fight or flight. Confidence lessens fear and deactivates this automatic survival mechanism.

In this "pause" there is room to deal with the potential threat in new ways. This is where teaching the young person nonviolent alternatives and conflict resolution skills comes into play. The mind that is not caught up in fear and therefore not caught up in the primitive fight or flight reaction, can think more clearly and intelligently and will come up with other methods of dealing with the problem that will open the possibility of ending conflict before it starts. The teaching of physical self-defense skills and intellectual conflict resolution skills together is organic. *One is dependent on the other.*

There is no doubt that the effects of these skills taught in youth will naturally have an effect on adult life. Understanding the fundamental causes of conflict as well as learning conflict resolution skills at an early age will also increase the chance of young people entering adulthood and approaching life with a more intelligent and nonviolent understanding of relationship. A young person taught to understand and deal with conflict knows instinctively that violence is not an acceptable way to solve the problems of relationship.

There is another issue related to the "fight or flight" reaction which is the mind's inability to distinguish between a physical or psychological threat. Hollywood has exploited Karate and the other martial arts by portraying them as lethal fighting.* This notion makes for a sensational appeal to our more primitive human responses. *All these violent images psychologically stimulate a fight or flight reaction even though the threat is not physically present.* In other words, the media's exposure of violent images triggers the mind/body's response as if the image were real — as if the image were an actual physical threat to our well being. With the constant stimulation of violent "life threatening" images, the brain is constantly on alert, using up a tremendous amount of energy to defend against a ghost of a threat — one that simply isn't there. Watching constant violence puts our "fight or flight" mechanism in a constant "on" mode, causing our bodies to continually produce chemical reactions to combat an invasion that in reality is not taking place.

---

*According to recent information, there are over 2,000,000 young people actually taking Karate in the United States alone. There are millions more that have been exposed to Karate through movies, magazines, and television. At public and private schools for which I've done demonstrations, almost all of the young people have seen Karate, but mostly the violent, Hollywood versions.

This response to such visual presentations creates tremendous fear. We are always on guard. It is not unusual to see global paranoia of "The Enemy." This feeling that everyone is out to get us, that we need to be constantly on guard, reinforces the feeling of isolation and separatism and our seeing ourselves as the psychological entities being threatened. *"I'm in danger!"* is the psychological response we get when images of violence create the fear of a real imminent physical threat. When the brain receives a psychological image of violence and interprets it as an actual physical threat, it reacts in a personal, psychological, defensive manner. It has a *psychological* flight or flight reaction.

In an actual combat situation when confronting a real danger to one's physical well being, one would need to actually fight or actually flee from the potential harm. But when the threat, via violent images, is merely psychological, then a physical fight or flight response is not appropriate. When this occurs, the brain goes through a mock fight or flight, playing out the scenario psychologically, which has the effect of producing heightened fear because the tension created by the supposed threat cannot be alleviated. This interpretation by the brain of greater fear provides even more justification that *"I am being threatened."*

This building up of individual fear develops and maintains the separate self, the psychological entity called the "ego." As I see it, the ego is made up in part of psychologically defensive reactions to threats, and through time and reinforcement develops its defensive self-protective positions of "I Versus You, Me Versus Them." In order to create and sustain itself, its self-protective power so to speak, it identifies with other more powerful images, that of the group, the nation, the culture, in an attempt to fortify its own like-minded core of defenses, which just leads to group fear, national isolation, and cultural conflict.

Thus, it seems to me that the brain's response to violent visual images portrayed on television, in the movies and in magazines can have a tremendously dangerous effect on behavior. I feel they are helping to create and sustain violence worldwide.

I'm not asking anyone to accept these statements as "truth," but rather as a working hypothesis, an insight into the nature and structure of violence. Each of you must decide for yourself if what has been said here is true or not. If it is true, then we have good reason to pursue inquiry into this urgent situation and develop contexts in which we can observe this actuality as it occurs. We must, in my view, not only teach children about conflict resolution at the symptomatic level but delve much deeper into what creates and sustains violence. Symptomatic resolving of conflict is reform and does not address the problem fundamentally.

In my view, Karate training is a unique way to help us understand violence and therefore can be a unique and successful way to deal intelligently with conflict resolution provided that both physical and mental skills are taught holistically — that is, together.

The need to help our children learn new solutions to violence is of paramount importance. As a parent, I feel it necessary to teach these skills in school, as well as in the community. It should be an integral part of the curriculum. Surely this issue dominates our lives more than, say, math or science alone. As a teacher, I know that it can be incorporated within the daily operation of classroom activities. Having been a school administrator, I know that programs combining a healthy discipline in Martial Arts training accompanied by developing nonviolent alternatives can be incorporated into the overall school structure. I am currently co-director of a private school that does exactly this. We use this approach in our school. And it works! Our teachers and parents see the need to teach conflict resolution, and understand how vital this need is. They know that children can be taught to successfully cope with violence in creative ways, because they have seen it happen.

If you are interested in more information on what we do, please feel free to contact us (our address is at the end of the book). Please let us know how your child or children responded to what I have written. This will be of great help to me in writing future books for young people on conflict resolution.

# About the Author

Terrence Webster-Doyle began his study of the martial arts in 1961, earning his black belt in the Japanese style of Gensei Ryu Karate from Sensei Shigeru Numano in 1967. Now a sixth-degree black belt, he is founder and director of the Martial Arts for Peace Association in Middlebury, Vermont.

Dr. Webster-Doyle earned his doctorate in health and human services and has taught at the secondary, community college, and university levels in education, psychology, and philosophy. He has worked in juvenile delinquency prevention and has developed conflict education programs for young people, combining principles from education, psychology, and the martial arts. Dr. Webster-Doyle's numerous books on martial arts, education, and social issues for young people and adults have won many awards for excellence.

# About the Artist

Rod Cameron was born in 1948 in Chicago, Illinois, but has lived in southern California most of his life. He studied painting with "Dick and Jane" illustrator Keith Ward, and at the Otis/Parson School of Design in Los Angeles.

In 1985, Rod Cameron founded East/West Arts, Inc., a design and art studio in Ventura, California. His work has been shown on major network television and has received awards for its illustrative excellence.

# International Praise
# for Dr. Terrence Webster-Doyle's Work

- Dr. Webster-Doyle has been awarded the Robert Burns Medal for Literature by Austria's Albert Schweitzer Society, for "outstanding merits in the field of peace promotion."

- "Dr. Webster-Doyle takes the reader beyond the physical aspects of Karate training to a discovery of self. These books are an asset to Martial Arts instructors, students and parents of all styles, ages and rank levels."

  —Marilyn Fierro, 5th Dan
  Owner and Chief Instructor
  Smithtown Karate Academy, Smithtown, NY

- Winner of Benjamin Franklin Awards for Excellence in Independent Publishing

- "These topics are excellent and highly relevant. If each of the major countries of the world were to have ten Drs. Webster-Doyle, world peace is guaranteed to be achieved over a period of just one generation."

  —Dr. Chas. Mercieca, Executive Vice-President
  International Ass'n of Educators for World Peace
  NGO, United Nations (ECOSOC), UNICEF & UNESCO

- Acclaimed at the Soviet Peace Fund Conference in Moscow and published in Russia by Moscow's Library of Foreign Literature and Magistr Publications.

- "Every publication from the pen of this author should make a significant contribution to peace within and without. Highly recommended!"

  —*New Age Publishers and Retailers Alliance Trade Journal*

- ***Why is Everybody Always Picking on Me?***—cited by the Omega New Age Directory as one of the Ten Best Books of 1991 for its "atmosphere of universal benevolence and practical application."

# Tales of the Empty-Handed Masters
## Classic Martial Arts Books for Young People
### by Dr. Terrence Webster-Doyle

The "Martial Arts for Peace" books offer young people a view of the Martial Arts as they should be seen: as a healthy and humane activity that can help them to live with sensitivity and intelligence in their daily lives.

## Can you discover the secret of the Empty-Handed Masters?

**BREAKING THE CHAINS OF THE ANCIENT WARRIOR.** This exciting new book depicts the profound mental and physical training of martial arts students. Through classic martial arts stories and the author's own experience, this book teaches the most important lesson of all: Respect.
*8-1/2 x 9-1/2; 172 pp; 22 color illustrations; $14.95 (pb)*

**EYE OF THE HURRICANE** embarks on the journey into the heart of "Empty Self," the path of self-confidence and nonviolent inner power.
*8-1/2 x 9-1/2; 128 pp; 20 color illustrations; $14.95 (pb)*

**MAZE OF THE FIRE DRAGON** travels further with symbolic challenges that lead the reader to understand his or her real strengths.
*8-1/2 x 9-1/2; 128 pp; 20 color illustrations; $14.95 (pb)*

**FLIGHT OF THE GOLDEN EAGLE** offers insights for understanding conflict, guiding the martial artist to live with awareness and intelligence.
*8-1/2 x 9-1/2; 112 pp; 20 color illustrations; $14.95 (pb)*